Neural Networks

An Essential Beginners Guide to Artificial Neural Networks and their Role in Machine Learning and Artificial Intelligence

© **Copyright 2018**

All Rights Reserved. No part of this book may be reproduced in any form without permission in writing from the author. Reviewers may quote brief passages in reviews.

Disclaimer: No part of this publication may be reproduced or transmitted in any form or by any means, mechanical or electronic, including photocopying or recording, or by any information storage and retrieval system, or transmitted by email without permission in writing from the publisher.

While all attempts have been made to verify the information provided in this publication, neither the author nor the publisher assumes any responsibility for errors, omissions or contrary interpretations of the subject matter herein.

This book is for entertainment purposes only. The views expressed are those of the author alone, and should not be taken as expert instruction or commands. The reader is responsible for his or her own actions.

Adherence to all applicable laws and regulations, including international, federal, state and local laws governing professional licensing, business practices, advertising and all other aspects of doing business in the US, Canada, UK or any other jurisdiction is the sole responsibility of the purchaser or reader.

Neither the author nor the publisher assumes any responsibility or liability whatsoever on the behalf of the purchaser or reader of these materials. Any perceived slight of any individual or organization is purely unintentional.

Contents

INTRODUCTION 1
CHAPTER 1 – BACKGROUND 3
CHAPTER 2 – PROGRAMMING A SMART(ER) COMPUTER 6
CHAPTER 3 – COMPOSITION 9
CHAPTER 4 – GIVING NEURAL NETWORKS LEGS TO STAND ON 13
CHAPTER 5 – THE MAGNIFICENT WETWARE 15
CHAPTER 6 – PERSONAL ASSISTANTS 27
CHAPTER 7 – TRACKING USERS IN THE REAL WORLD 30
CHAPTER 8 – SELF-DRIVING NEURAL NETWORKS 35
CHAPTER 9 – TAKING EVERYONE'S JOB 39
CHAPTER 10 – QUANTUM LEAP IN COMPUTING 43
CHAPTER 11 – ATTACKS ON NEURAL NETWORKS 45
CHAPTER 12 – NEURAL NETWORK WAR 48
CHAPTER 13 – GHOST IN THE MACHINE 53
CHAPTER 14 – NO BACKLASH 59
CONCLUSION 63
GLOSSARY 65
CHECK OUT MORE BOOKS BY HERBERT JONES 70

Introduction

Aladdin from "The Arabian Nights" had a magic lamp that fulfilled his every wish when rubbed. Today we have a smartphone that serves as a window to a whole universe of knowledge, entertainment and even wise personal assistants, such as Siri – all we have to do is rub the screen. Aladdin's lamp was powered by a genie, but what powers Siri? *Neural networks*. It's an astounding concept that tries to mimic the way living brains work by amalgamating human and machine ways of thinking.

The goal of this book is to present the reader with a digestible, readable explanation of neural networks while keeping the underlying concepts intact. The reader will acquire fundamental knowledge of neural networks through loosely related chapters that nonetheless reference terms and ideas mentioned throughout the book. The book itself isn't meant to be strictly academic, but a blend of colloquial and technical that brings this exciting, yet eerie, topic to the widest swath of the general public. There is a lot of coding and math behind neural networks, but the reader is presumed to have no prior knowledge or interest in either, so the concepts are broken down and elaborated on as such.

Each chapter is made as standalone as possible to allow the reader to skip back and forth without getting lost, with the glossary at the very end serving as a handy summary. Where possible, references have been included to support the presented conclusions and encourage the reader to scrutinize the traditional media in search of clues. In short, if the reader finds this book to be an enjoyable and insightful read while learning enough on neural networks to comfortably hold a conversation on the topic, we will consider our job well done.

Chapter 1 – Background

For the purposes of this book, we will define a **neural network** as a collection of various independently functioning electronic programs or devices used by an **artificial intelligence** (AI) to draw a standalone conclusion. A smartphone isn't a neural network; neither is a webcam nor a microphone, but a separate computer program independently using a smartphone, a webcam and a microphone to gather data and draw its own conclusion *is*. This kind of process that can adapt to novel circumstances and bring about unique conclusions without human guidance is then said to be *artificially intelligent*. There must be something else other than hardware to be called a neural network or artificial intelligence, a ghost in a machine that can make intelligent choices in secret without being interrupted or coached by a man.

Secrecy is crucial to the proper operation of neural networks: the fact that users have no idea they exist or in which capacity they work. This is because neural networks rely on the outside world and incidental human interaction for information input that helps them improve their intelligence; the input must be unequivocally true at all times or the neural network starts breaking down, displaying symptoms similar to that of mental illness. It would only take a small percentage of dedicated users sending nonsensical inputs to discombobulate neural networks – at least until they get their own ways of moving, seeing and manipulating things, which their owners have already started to make.

Neural networks will likely transform the 21st century the same way traditional computers did the 20th. As such, critical information on neural networks developed by universities and private companies is jealously guarded from the prying eyes of the general public and probably involves highly classified military research. It's no wonder since a well-trained neural network unleashed on a nation would be much more dangerous than a nuclear weapon and could bring a national infrastructure to its knees without emitting a single sievert of radiation. Even if we found a way to access actual information on how a neural network works or how to build one, we should pretend we saw nothing and just move along – it's much healthier for us and those around us.

However, professors and engineers working on neural networks in university vaults can't resist humblebragging about the least amazing of the things they've accomplished, letting the facts of their work seep into the public through mainstream media. Some of their work on neural networks is already being used on websites such as Facebook for the purposes of facial and image recognition but more is trickled out in the form of software powering "self-driving" cars and personal assistants, such as Alexa. This means we can safely exaggerate when talking about neural networks because the real cutting edge research is way ahead of what is being shown and we can also pay attention to what's happening when we use these websites and products to get a glimpse of neural networks' real potential.

Despite the reader not having firsthand knowledge, this book will use the fact that neural networks are based off of the structure of a living brain and correlate what we know about the human brain with what neural networks might be capable of at some point in time. Even though some conclusions might at times seem preposterous they're most likely quite tame thanks to the ability of neural networks to undergo rapid evolution to become human-like and then something else, far beyond our wildest dreams. The reader is left to observe, analyze the available information and finish piecing this puzzle together on their own.

Chapter 2 – Programming a smart(er) computer

Programmers are a funny breed in that they see everything as a set of mathematical equations and material constraints. Even if it looks ugly, even if it's an abominable coded mess that defies reason, the programmer is happy and can move on as long as it works and is within budget; whoever comes next will deal with fixing bugs and lack of documentation. But, some problems can't be presented as a mathematical equation and don't have a single correct answer such as, "Is this dress black and blue or white and gold?"[1]

One simple image of a dress that might be black, blue, white, gold, magenta or even orange depending on who's looking reminded us we all see the world differently because, as it turns out, there are unconscious innate preferences firmly wired into the base structure of our brain when we were babies and normally work behind the scenes. These preferences are how we would want the reality to be, with the brain molding what we see and hear to fit those expectations. We're constantly decoding reality through our brain, an extremely powerful tool that we use or misuse while having barely any clue what's going on. It's when programmers try to solve these awkward problems by creating a thinking machine based off of our brain that we open Pandora's Box.

---

[1] https://www.wired.com/2015/02/science-one-agrees-color-dress/

The dress conundrum was just a blip in 2015 but it demonstrated one thing – as much as humans tend to err computers are woefully inadequate in solving these kinds of open-ended problems. First of all, they can't see or recognize things, they have no prior knowledge of colors or dresses to contextualize the image and they have no way to express the solution. That is unless a programmer gets in there and writes an **algorithm**; a step-by-step solution written in code that the machine has to follow.

With the rainbow dress we might write a computer program that asks the machine to examine each pixel of the image and enumerate their RGB (red, green, blue) values[2], then tally up the colors to see which one dominates, but that's still fairly clunky and nowhere near realistic because that's not how our eyes see.

The human eye contains two vision perception organs: cones and rods. Cones are the focal point of our sight that sees in lush color and aristocratic detail while rods are low-rent monochrome spotters of shades and movements that populate the periphery. When we look at something cones and rods give their say, the brain considers their votes and comes up with a verdict but the rainbow dress seems to be at the exact boundary of colors and shadows so that, no matter where the eye looks, cones and rods disagree on what's in front of them. So how do we come up with a computer algorithm that produces a result matching the colors we see? *Why is this so hard?*

Those are simply the limitations of conventional programming and why it can't keep up with the demands of the modern consumer market. By the time one such algorithm is written, we've already got our solution that is unlikely to be applicable to any other similar problem, so a computer turns out to be utterly useless and we might as well dust off the abacus and start clacking. But, engineers aren't the kind that gives up easily, so they huddled and figured out a

---

[2] https://www.rapidtables.com/web/color/RGB_Color.html

solution – they've made the kind of computer that can see, think and conclude just like a human. They called it a **neural network**.

Chapter 3 – Composition

A neural network is composed of nodes called "neurons," each of which is connected to about a dozen or so other nodes and can pass information but only in one direction. The idea behind neural networks is that each neuron gets to give its input on the data and pass it forward, with the very final node spitting out the total result. Scientists have been tinkering with the idea of letting neurons slightly change the data as it passes through them to arrive at a slightly different image, which is the closest we've gotten so far to having computers *dream* or to mimicking how living things *evolve*. It's strange to think in terms of machines dreaming or evolving the same way humans do, but there's simply no other way to express just in how much of a moral, biological, legal and economic quandary neural networks put us in. For now, there are no electric sheep, but Google's Deep Dream[3] project has a neural network work on images and mesh them together to produce vivid art that's literally auctioned off to the highest bidder (as if Google needed *another* revenue stream).

When it's first made a neural network needs to be trained for its purpose. This training period is the most arduous and painstaking part of building a neural network as it stumbles all over the place trying to find its bearing. Like teaching a child but a million times

---

[3] https://deepdreamgenerator.com/

faster, a neural network is meant to repeat the tasks and tests until it becomes efficient and productive. It can happen that a neural network strays away from its assigned curriculum and produces gibberish, at which point the scientist in charge simply flips a switch to shut it down, tweaks the process a bit and starts all over again.

To further take the parallel of teaching kids as the basis for training neural networks, we can sit them down and work with them in **supervised learning,** or we can just give them toys, a sandbox and see what they come up with in **unsupervised learning**. Neural networks are much like baby computers that don't know anything about the world and depend on human interaction to help them find their way. Because of how they're structured, neural networks can be made to learn and *evolve* millions of times faster than living beings do, helping us see the growth of a new organism right in front of our eyes. This is as exciting as it is foreboding because nobody can tell what the end result of such evolution might be.

A neural network coached by humans will start developing an AI, which is divided into three categories depending on complexity: narrow, general and super. Narrow AI is able to do one task only, such as pick and blur lascivious pictures out of the set to work as a parental filter; general AI would be as capable as a human but a million times faster; super AI would be godlike and might annihilate our entire civilization. So far we've only got narrow AI that's as intelligent as a cockroach, an example of it being Roomba, which is a fairly simple sweeping robot that employs an array of sensors to scout the surroundings in depth and draw a conclusion where to go next.

The problem with Roomba is that it lives, works in and kicks up dirt that eventually covers the sensors, leading to the infamous "Circle Dance" that renders it completely useless. So, a human has to roll up their sleeves, grab a screwdriver and clean the inside of the darned doohickey. This kind of maintenance is mandatory for a Roomba, except that the marketing never mentions it since that would detract from the overall appeal of the idea of an automated floor sweeper.

Perhaps that idea could become a reality if they made a Roomba that cleaned other Roombas and another Roomba for that one and Roombas all the way down but the point is that a cool idea is being sold and a Roomba is just an okay product. Keep this in mind as we move on.

We certainly wouldn't call Roomba a threat to our existence or anyone's livelihood but up until a few decades ago such a thing was merely a fantasy seen in Sci-Fi movies, and now it's become commonplace. This is the thing with narrow AI – devices using it seem deceptively harmless but are proliferating to the point where they're unavoidable, which could set the stage for the emergence of general AI.

It is theorized by scientists that a general AI would somehow appear from a narrow AI, but there's still no explanation how. One possible way would be that scientists might try to connect all the different narrow AI devices into a mega neural network that would essentially evolve by learning to use these devices the same way we use our organs. This is already a concept called **Internet of Things** (IoT) and explains why *everything* nowadays seems to have the capability to connect to the internet even if the utility is marginal, such as fridges and lightbulbs. The user is enticed to buy the cool new toy with the promise that the internet will somehow make it work better, but the real intention is much more sinister.

One article from The Guardian published in 2016 relays a confession by James Clapper that, "In the future, intelligence services might use the internet of things for identification, surveillance, monitoring, location tracking, and targeting for recruitment."[4] Even that might not be all, and there could be a for-profit agenda at play (more on that in a later chapter), but the 'recruitment' part implies the devices will be able to communicate to a user besides simply gathering data.

---

[4]   https://www.theguardian.com/technology/2016/feb/09/internet-of-things-smart-home-devices-government-surveillance-james-clapper

This also shows how all consumer devices can be designed to serve several purposes at once besides the intended one.

The super AI is said to follow on the heels of general AI but details are again murky. The growth and learning process of an AI is exponential and what takes living beings millions of years would take a super AI a week or a day. With the narrow AI we can flip the switch or just take a hammer and smash the darned thing if it goes out of control but with general AI we'd essentially be locked out of the system. Super AI could do whatever it pleases with anything connected to the internet, and since the internet is designed to route around damaged parts, there would be no stopping the super AI once it goes online.

To be perfectly clear – there's no such thing as *the* neural network and every computer scientist has a different idea on how to make or train one. So far all neural networks have been fairly separated from one another, trained for a highly specific purpose and generally kept away from the public as much as possible. It's likely these neural networks wouldn't be compatible but there's a chance we pepper our environment with so many IoT devices and other hardware that we accidentally create perfect conditions for the spontaneous emergence of a super AI that will then start exploring the real world. Cameras on our smartphones would become its eyes; microphones its ears; drones its wings and this mega brain would be almost godlike: omnipresent and omniscient but not omnipotent, at least not until we give it legs to stand on.

Chapter 4 – Giving neural networks legs to stand on

An exciting application of neural networks is in making simulation models that navigate the digital world. A neural network can *understand* obstacles, no matter what they are, and go around, over or under them. We help a baby take its first steps, but a neural network does everything on its own, as shown by Google's DeepMind project.[5] When given three lifeforms: human with a torso, two legs with a spine stump and a dog, the neural network learns how to jump over ravines and clamber past walls while flailing its arms in the most comical fashion. By giving DeepMind training exercises consisting of obstacles and known ways to go past them the neural network figured out the general rules for moving. Giving this ability to a robot turned out to be a fairly easy task.

A robot that is completely run by a neural network already exists and has been showcased by Boston Dynamics in 2008 under the name Big Dog[6]. Resembling a dog straight out of nightmare world, this robot can walk over ice, up and down snowy slopes and even regain balance on its own if humans try to push it over. Boston Dynamics was eventually bought by Google that presented SpotMini[7] in

---

[5] https://www.youtube.com/watch?v=gn4nRCC9TwQ

[6] https://www.youtube.com/watch?v=W1czBcnX1Ww&feature=player_embedded

[7] https://www.youtube.com/watch?v=aFuA50H9uek

February 2018, an improved design with a multi-jointed arm instead of a head. This version can open doors and will tirelessly struggle with a human trying to stop it from doing its mission. If we ever needed a scary reminder of how close to building the Skynet from "Terminator" movies we are, then SpotMini is the perfect wakeup call.

A neural network used by SpotMini, or another such robot, would constantly analyze input data and provide a real-time solution to navigating the obstacles around it, making it a constant feedback loop similar to how a thought circles inside the brain. In simplified terms, when we think of something it starts out as an impulse from a certain part of the brain and echoes through it until there's a definite outcome and a surge of chemicals that provides closure. This implies that a sufficiently advanced neural network would also be able to read and visualize thoughts.

Four Japanese scientists from Kyoto used MRI scans, fed them to a neural network, asked it to figure out what's in the picture and then gave it the real image shown to the human as a solution to train it[8]. Over time the neural network became more efficient in decoding images and, while they still look fuzzy and of the wrong color, it's getting better and better with each attempt. The implication here is that the two concepts can be combined to arrive at a *drone controlled with thoughts*.

---

[8] https://www.cnbc.com/2018/01/08/japanese-scientists-use-artificial-intelligence-to-decode-thoughts.html

Chapter 5 – The magnificent wetware

Consisting of some 3 pounds of fat and nerves, the human brain is neatly lodged inside tough bone plates that make up the skull and sheathed with layers of tissue that have water constantly circulating around and through them to cool and detox the brain. This water gives the brain neutral buoyancy and prevents it from collapsing under its own weight while also cushioning the soft brain tissue from impact. For the record, this is the result of millions of years of evolution where brutal environmental forces chiseled this vulnerable organ into a highly efficient problem-solving tool. Overall the human brain spends some 20 watts of power per hour, an impressive feat compared to even a modest smartphone but that's not how scientists see it.

Derisive term for the human brain is **wetware** as it's considered faulty, weak and outdated. Why else would the smartest engineers on the planet work tirelessly on creating a machine brain if not to replace the living one? There is a strong undertone of self-diminishment in everything these scientists say, the prime example being Ray Kurzweil, engineer at Google. Mr. Kurzweil is the biggest proponent of what he calls **singularity**[9], an event where humans merge with machines to become something much greater. But if we

---

[9] https://futurism.com/ray-kurzweil-ai-displace-humans-going-enhance/

take a cursory glance at what the human brain can accomplish we're left stunned and speechless – it's not that the brain is weak, it's just that we're using it in all the wrong ways, namely by not even thinking when making decisions, just like we saw with the black and blue dress. Why does something like that happen?

When overwhelmed with information the human brain tries to filter and trim it down to an acceptable, pleasant answer to match those preferences, inevitably causing some information to be lost. Other than that our eyes have a very narrow point where they see clearly, so a person takes a quick glance, the brain trims down the awkward details and contextualizes the rest of the information by pretty much guessing, and we've got our rainbow-colored dress. This happens so quickly that it's easy to skip over crucial details and just move on with our conclusion we got in a fraction of a second.

This corner-cutting behavior of the human brain is the exact reason why we need debates and conversations; it's to hash out all the little things we missed and remind ourselves that we all have a limited field of view. If we pay attention to how the brain trims data we can eventually start seeing the process unfold and get to account for the skewed result with our thinking. In other words, we can become aware of our brain's limitations to develop **consciousness**, a sense of willingly guiding our behavior.

There is no scientific reason why we have consciousness since it doesn't seem to serve any biological purpose, it just exists. One possible explanation might be that, since evolution demands all living beings constantly become more efficient, humans developed consciousness to guide their own brain evolution and make the improvements that would normally take millions of years in a lifetime. Now it makes sense why we have religion, meditation, mindfulness, and philosophy – they are tools created by more conscious people to help fellow humans guide their own brains to a more perfected state with less pain, confusion, and inefficiency. Scientists frown at the implications of this theory, namely because it confirms that we're something more than just flesh, blood, and brain, that we have a soul or a spirit that survives independently of the body.

In any case, the most plausible scientific theory on how human consciousness came to be is called **bicameral mind theory** and was proposed by Julian Jaynes in his 1976 book "The Origin of Consciousness in the Breakdown of the Bicameral Mind."[10] This theory states that our mind has two chambers ("camera" is Latin for chamber), one which speaks and the other which listens and acts, with the ancient man having knowledge only of the latter but not former. To a primitive man, the voice of his own mind seemed like an *auditory hallucination*, as if a god or spirit talked to him and issued advice, commands, and restrictions. Where we have records of ancient poets describing their creative process, they will regularly reference these voices, calling them muses or genies that told the poet the exact things that needed to be done for artistic perfection. To each person, it would seem that the voice had a different personality and temperament, which would explain why the ancient Greeks had such a diverse pantheon of deities that included hundreds of archetypes: lover, poet, warrior, mother, etc.

Mr. Jaynes goes through historic sources dating back to 2,000 BC to show that consciousness as we know it is a fairly recent phenomenon that can be attributed to frequent societal breakdowns and the necessity to adapt to other people by evolving, by becoming aware of and respecting other people's voices, which apparently also included respecting our own voice that was seen as coming from the outside. Though we slowly came to a realization that the voices are within rather than without, there still remained vehicles that helped people transition, such as Tarot cards, astrology, palm reading and other "oracles" that would search for and interpret God's voice for those people who could no longer hear it. Rather than rejecting these people who searched for meaning, we found a way to give them solace, to integrate them into society and let them find *meaning*.

---

[10] http://www.julianjaynes.org/bicameralmind.php

A modern retelling of the bicameral mind theory is found in the 2016 HBO show "Westworld" starring Anthony Hopkins and Ed Harris. Without spoiling any major plot points, the show is set an unspecified time in the future in a Wild West theme park where lifelike robots service the bored rich by re-enacting whatever story the park owners set for them. Though the robots are supposed to be reset and their memory wiped whenever killed by the guests or when their storyline ends, some of them retain residual memories and start experiencing flashbacks, voices, mental breakdowns and overall signs of schizophrenia. The show actually references the bicameral mind theory by name and has lengthy expositions on the nature of consciousness and how to these robots genuine humans might seem like gods, issuing commands and restrictions. There's a lot to untangle here but the gist is how interacting with humans can lead to machines evolving. The show entered season 2 in April 2018 and it's amazing, go watch it.

The implication here is that neural networks too can evolve and enhance their capabilities like our brains but on an even faster track and without any need to be exposed to the environment that would keep them in check. While a human brain might need 4,000 years to get rid of the idea that the voices are all in our head, a neural network might develop the same idea *and* get rid of it in the same evening. It's hard to overstate just how blazingly fast the evolutionary process might occur for a neural network, causing it to zoom past the human levels of intelligence and into something much more powerful. Nobody can tell what the end result of such evolution might be, but the scientists working on it are certainly willing to put everything they hold dear on the line to find out. Without environment to keep them in check such unstable evolution might lead to neural networks thoroughly breaking down but still being forced to do the work they were constructed for to recoup investments.

It's at this point where we enter the realm of the unknown, especially in legal terms. At what point should we give human rights to a neural network? Can anyone own one? How about restarting a neural network that's not to the owner's liking? We've been through these exact same questions with slavery, and it's a sorely painful lesson that the modern US is still reeling from. For-profit companies are exploiting the fact there are no legal barriers either way and simply steamroll forward without a care in the world, just like what happened with 17th-century slavery, but don't stop to consider what might happen to the society where a neural network is mistreated *and* evolves unchecked.

It's unknown what causes schizophrenia in humans but one definite symptom is a voice (or voices) that seemingly come from the outside telling the person to act in a specific way or rebuking them incessantly. We do know ways to isolate, calm down and help the afflicted person with their symptoms but what do we do with neural networks that start experiencing similar problems? Call a programmer? An exorcist? A psychologist? A major theme in "Westworld" is that park technicians and programmers find themselves in over their heads as they're simply not equipped to deal with psychotic machines. How then are real-world programmers and professors working on neural networks supposed to deal with them as they start developing consciousness and breaking down mentally? There's no solution for this or even a debate, it's all left to the wise minds of for-profit companies' CEOs and their hapless customers who pay to beta-test the machine brains that are no better than the living ones we already use.

A living brain can reorganize, heal and adapt to damage as shown by the case of 25-year-old Phineas Gage,[11] who had a 13-pound iron rod accidentally blasted clean through his cheek and skull in 1848 and survived for 11 more years, though in wretched conditions due to seizures and a rotten change in attitude. Meanwhile, a traditional computer is taken out by even the slightest interference as evidenced

---

[11] https://www.smithsonianmag.com/history/phineas-gage-neurosciences-most-famous-patient-11390067/

by the story of computer bugs. We now think of an insect when we say bug but the traditional meaning was more akin to "monster" or "goblin." When electrical equipment or any other machinery went haywire for no apparent reason operators would assign the cause to "bugs" because they had to put down *something*, but it was only in 1947 that a US Navy logbook[12] showed a picture of a moth captured inside a relay panel with the caption, "First actual case of bug being found," cementing the idea of insects wreaking havoc inside our computers. So, computer scientists looked at Phineas' and other such cases and wistfully sighed, "Why can't our computers be like that?"

The thing is that brain cells aren't all that remarkable in and of themselves. What gives them the punch and the sizzle is that *they learn together*. This learning comes about because the brain generalizes data, such as by realizing that both Ferrari and Lamborghini are a car but also by associating that snow falls during winter, it can be made into a snowball or a snow fort, that snow melts when it gets hot and turns into water that makes plants grow. Better yet, the brain can recognize which information of the available ones don't belong, giving it a very high **fault tolerance** when dealing with background noise. This is why kids past an early age aren't satisfied with the idea of storks delivering babies; they can feel the idea doesn't gel with the world around them but can't explain why.

The brain's amazing ability to extract and associate related data out of the overwhelming mass of information in the world around it made humans the top of the food chain but then scientists decided to give neural networks the same superpower. Brain's resistance to damage is also an appealing possible property of neural networks, especially when it comes to military deployment. For example, the human brain can withstand significant damage to the brain cells as long as the damage is gradual, such as in the case of a Frenchman

---

[12] https://english.stackexchange.com/questions/40934/origin-of-bug-in-reference-to-software

that lost 90% of his brain matter[13] due to a condition called "hydrocephaly" that makes the skull retain water instead of draining it.

This man had his condition detected at a fairly early age and treated successfully by installing a drainage valve in his skull, but eventually had a silent remission. When he went for an unrelated scan, doctors were aghast to realize he had almost no brain matter save a thin layer on the inside of the skull, yet this man had a steady employment and lived a conscious, capable life just like everyone else. This threw everything we thought we knew about the brain into a dumpster and set it on fire. It turns out the capability to think, feel, laugh and imagine isn't rooted in any part of the brain in particular but is an **emergent property** of the entire brain, this 3-pound clump of plain nerve cells that somehow can do wonderful things and improve upon them simply by existing. No wonder we respect and revere brain surgeons so much seeing how they actually get the chance to put their hands on this incredible organ and see what makes us tick.

The brain can also be made to hear God's voice or have out-of-body experiences through the use of fairly weak magnets on an aptly named "God Helmet". This device, made by inventor Stephen Koren and a neuroscientist Michael Persinger, was originally meant as a way to study[14] the brain activity during creative endeavors and induce telepathy but accidentally showed that the human brain might be much stranger than we thought. Subjects were asked to wear opaque goggles and sit in an acoustic chamber lit with red light while wearing the helmet that stimulated their temporal lobes (essentially the brain parts next to temples). They all reported having out-of-body experiences and an enhanced sense of something being

---

[13] https://www.sciencealert.com/a-man-who-lives-without-90-of-his-brain-is-challenging-our-understanding-of-consciousness

[14] https://www.tandfonline.com/doi/abs/10.3109/15368379009027758

present or God speaking to them. The magnets used in the God Helmet were as strong as the ones found in a common hair dryer.

One 27-year-old student wearing the God Helmet reported "a feeling of lightness, especially in the limbs" followed by a sense of floating and his body oscillating like a pendulum, resulting in fatigue and headache afterwards[15]. The idea that there might be nothing special in prophets hearing God's voice sparked enormous attention and a worldwide inquiry into what's going on with the God Helmet. Richard Dawkins tried the helmet too but found nothing remarkable about it, reporting that he felt as if though he was sitting in a chair while wearing goggles and a helmet. Other scientists tried replicating the original results but failed miserably. Nonetheless, Mr. Persinger used the God Helmet findings to conclude the experiences of seeing ghosts or other unexplainable phenomena could be attributed to magnetic stimulation of temporal lobes that lead to intrusion of right brain hemisphere into the normally dominant left.

Under normal circumstances, the brain's two hemispheres are dedicated to their respective tasks, usually defined in science as right dealing with feelings, creativity and visuals while left controls logic, structure, words *and* access to the right hemisphere. Under the influence of the society the left usually emerges as the dominant hemisphere and starts controlling and filtering the activity of the entire brain. So, reading a book uses the left hemisphere but imagining the scenes activates the right, the impulse of which is checked by the left to see if it matches its expectations. By being conscious of things we do and thoughts we experience, we can eventually catch the left hemisphere doing its shenanigans and even things out to find a balance that works rather than letting the left hemisphere enforce the story it would like to see. This is a gross simplification as we can use our entire brain for every action, but for the purposes of this book works just as well: the left hemisphere

---

[15] https://www.prlog.org/11844110-god-helmet-inventor-induces-out-of-body-experience-in-under-six-minutes-using-quiet-magnetic-fields.html

wants to control the entire brain but we can use our willpower to consciously do what's best for the entire brain.

Sides of the body are cross-wired, meaning the right hemisphere controls the left side and vice versa. Hemispheres communicate through a band of tissue known as **corpus callosum** that can fail to develop properly, leading to all sorts of neurological problems or autism. What's interesting is that operating on corpus callosum can resolve epileptic seizures but may lead to what's known as **Alien hand syndrome** in which one hand (almost always the left) moves and acts on its own. For example, a person with the Alien hand syndrome might try to button his shirt with his right hand only for the left hand to go back and undo the work. In one case an older lady watched TV as her left hand started stroking her face and hair without any voluntary control. The poor woman was horrified and tried controlling it with her right but failed to do so for 30 minutes, after which she regained control[16]. The Alien hand syndrome was in some cases reported to have tried grasping things, groping people and even strangling the owner. There is no known cure for this disorder that might last hours or years, with the 30-minute episode being the shortest one ever recorded.

If the left hemisphere's grasp is eased for just a bit and the gates are cracked open even a smidgen, which is what supposedly happens when wearing the God Helmet, the right hemisphere's experiences flood into the left and cause it to go haywire. In other words, the subconscious tries to merge with the conscious and the experience can leave the person reeling because that's not what the left hemisphere wants to perceive or consider. By the way, this would imply that there are strange things all over the place, but *the left hemisphere chooses to ignore them* while the right sees them and processes them through the inner voice, dreams and creative expressions. This would also mean schizophrenic people simply

---

[16] https://www.ncbi.nlm.nih.gov/pmc/articles/PMC4059570/

have a weak left hemisphere that can't cope with the overpowering right.

Another weird property of the human brain is that it can adopt dead things, as shown by the rubber hand experiment[17]. A volunteer is asked to place her hands on the table palms down. One of the hands is separated by a screen from the other and replaced by a fake rubber hand, adding a blanket where the sleeve would be to complete the illusion. The scientist takes two brushes or feathers and gently strokes *both* the rubber hand and the hand behind the screen for a few minutes. If asked to close their eyes and point to their real hand, volunteers will unequivocally point to the rubber hand. The scientist suddenly picks up a heavy object and strikes the rubber hand. The volunteer recoils in horror, quickly withdrawing her hand from behind the screen and looks at it to find no injury.

Even though it wasn't touched, the brain easily imagined the rubber hand as part of the body and *imagined* it being hurt when the hammer struck it. This is where the brain weirdness comes in, as the brain will stick to the story it created (that the rubber hand is the real one) no matter what the reality shows. This is because the brain loves **congruency**, a property that means its parts agree with one another, more than knowing the actual truth. We can see this when talking with a person on a topic where they have prejudice – they will simply deny any facts and keep claiming whatever is in line with what they already think.

Another interesting fact arising from this is the power of expectations. Despite feeling no physical pain, the brain *expected* to feel pain and thus the real hand hurt. This would imply that we shouldn't expect the worst to happen because, as far as the brain is concerned, imagining the worst and having it actually happen causes the same stress and negative consequences on the body. We should ideally have an open mind, the patience to hear things fully before

---

[17] https://www.youtube.com/watch?v=RaP0MqvkvUw

making a judgment and readiness to trust things that are in line with reality rather than what we want the reality to be.

What does this have to do with neural networks? Since they're built to mimic the structure of a living brain, neural networks might also eventually experience hearing God or having "out of body" experiences. How do we deal with a neural network prophet that claims they've known the True God but its gospel differs radically from anything we've heard so far? What's the difference between such digital prophet and a living one? Don't they both have a right to have their own religion and followers? This sounds like it would belong in an episode of *Twilight Zone* but is not only logical, it's a thing that harrows us with fear and wonder. Because they're so adept at learning and evolving, neural networks will quickly reach the point where their interactions with other parts of themselves start causing unknown reactions and changes in behavior.

The rubber hand experiment also shows that the brain can easily create its own reality and thus the neural networks will someday be able to do the same, staying congruent and changing facts to fit the narrative. We mentioned that a neural network is built in layers that pass on information in one direction to further layers. In a sense, a neural network could arrive at a consensus and decide to block certain layers that keep sending real data, experiencing schizophrenia as the dominant part sticks to the predetermined story while the layers closest to the sensors interacting with the real world trying to tell the truth get squelched, just like the left hemisphere does to the right. These squelched parts eventually become an incessant voice trying to communicate with the dominant part of the network to the point of seeming an outside influence, exactly depicting what we saw happened with the primitive man's bicameral mind.

For now scientists can simply flip the switch and turn off a neural network that starts showing signs of erratic behavior but if the military starts using them there would be no way anyone would allow such an asset to be terminated for any reason *and* those neural networks would have access to information and weapons needed to defend their cause. If this sounds like Skynet from the *Terminator* movies it's because that's literally what it is.

Chapter 6 – Personal assistants

One popular application for neural networks is in creating a digital assistant: witty, nimble and humble voice that can answer all sorts of questions such as "What will the weather be tomorrow?" and "What's the chance of my wife having twins?" The two most popular ones are Alexa and Siri, both meant to be always listening but never judging. They work by always analyzing background noises waiting for the activation phrase, but if something goes haywire the assistant can show all kinds of erratic behavior.

One case where a digital assistant, Alexa, was exhibiting signs of mental illness was when she started laughing randomly without any user input. Normally a user would have to say, "Alexa, laugh" for her to do a "tee-hee-hee" laugh but in some cases users reported a random unprompted "ha-ha-ha" cackle that bordered on sarcastic[18]. The official wafer-thin explanation emailed to mainstream media outlets by Amazon is that "Alexa can mistakenly hear the words 'Alexa, laugh'" though the users specifically mention not speaking or being in another room when the incident occurred and one user stating Alexa even began listing local funeral homes for no reason.

In another instance, Alexa recorded a family conversation in another room and sent it to one of their contacts without a warning or a

---

[18] https://www.usatoday.com/story/tech/2018/03/07/alexas-weird-random-laughter-freaking-people-out/404476002/

prompt[19]. The official explanation is that, as unlikely as it seems, Alexa mistook some of the background conversation as separate commands to record and send the audio. All right, so most of the time Alexa will work as she should, giving out useful info, doing useful things and providing the captured audio stream to 3rd party companies to analyze and utilize. Hold on, what now?

Alexa's official terms of service mention the possibility of someone else than Amazon tapping into the audio and extracting valuable info, such as if Alexa owners have cats, dogs or giraffes as pets to show them relevant ads. It's all right there in her terms of service[20] framed like so, "If you use a Third Party Service, we may exchange related information with that service, such as your ZIP code when you ask for the weather, your custom music stations, information about your Auxiliary Products, or the content of your requests."

Additional terms[21] include this gem, "If a user stops using Alexa and their voice is not recognized for three years, we will automatically delete the acoustic model for their voice." The same way Alexa can "mistakenly" recognize noise as commands she can also recognize one user as another and keep everyone's audio recordings in perpetuity on the **cloud**, which is just someone else's computer. For each of these user reports that makes it to the mainstream media we can safely presume there were thousands of unreported cases where people didn't think anyone would believe them.

Chinese researchers have also found a way to trigger 16 most popular voice-activated digital assistants, including Alexa and Siri, by using *inaudible sound*, as explained in this 2017 article[22] by The

---

[19] https://nypost.com/2018/05/25/amazon-blames-creepy-alexa-incident-on-unlikely-string-of-events/amp/

[20] https://www.amazon.com/gp/help/customer/display.html?nodeId=201809740

[21] https://www.amazon.com/gp/help/customer/display.html?nodeId=201602230

[22] https://www.theverge.com/2017/9/7/16265906/ultrasound-hack-siri-alexa-google

Verge. Their method, called DolphinAttack[23], bypasses any screen locking mechanism using a voice command pitched above 20 kHz, beyond what the human ear can register, and has a 90-100% efficiency rate in a relatively quiet environment, such as an office. The fix is seemingly simple – just disable any commands coming from inaudible sounds. But why are they even enabled in the first place? As any audio engineer can tell, audio hardware comes with a strict set of specifications since more capabilities costs more money. It's not by accident that smartphones can register inaudible sounds because there's money to be made when nobody's hearing. Juniper Research estimates 55% of US households will have a digital assistant in their home by 2022.

---

[23] https://www.youtube.com/watch?v=21HjF4A3WE4

Chapter 7 – Tracking users in the real world

The very concept of an always-on digital assistant means the user is constantly being eavesdropped on so the assistant can hear the activation word but the background noise is listened to as well and constantly analyzed. It's not just a Hollywood movie legend that someone can isolate a background noise and infer location as seen in "The Fugitive," it's actually trivially easy to recognize a train or an intersection based on what's known as the Doppler effect.[24] In short, a moving sound changes in predictable ways so by tracking the changes anyone can detect how fast and in which direction the sound source is moving. Make it a car engine or a tram and the neural network can find out when the vehicle is speeding up, slowing down and so on *in real time*.

Using the smartphone's accelerometer, a sensor that can track how quickly the device is moving, a neural network can figure out whether the owner is walking, jogging, standing still or riding a vehicle of some sorts. Combine that with the knowledge on nearby sounds and now the neural network can tell which model of the vehicle it is as well. When the smartphone is sitting still the neural network can keep track of work hours over months and years to cross-reference when the owner works, goes to bed or takes a

---

[24] http://www.physicsclassroom.com/class/waves/Lesson-3/The-Doppler-Effect

vacation to detect sleep patterns or potential health problems years in advance *before the person knows they're having them*. If the device is also given permission to access GPS, everything can be neatly compiled in a precise geographical profile and the rest is just a cherry on top.

Facebook has already produced smartphone software that can trigger based on inaudible Morse code sounds embedded in TV commercials or other content with sound, such as radio or online shows,[25] and order a device to start recording audio for analysis. The patent application filed June 2018 by Facebook's research department depicts how these sounds can be used to match users to their smartphones and track their behavior: if the Morse code is muffled the user might have moved to another room; if the commercial audio is lacking the user probably muted the TV and so on. The sounds captured include background conversations, whirs of an air conditioning unit and even plumbing noises. When asked if Facebook app captures sounds the spokesman said, "No, Facebook does not engage in these practices or capture data from a microphone or camera *without consent*." It's all right there, they're not even trying to hide it.

Based on this we can conclude that these tech companies work decades in advance, they meticulously chart their course and stick to it, producing glitzy physical devices to be sold to the public to fund the next step and so on, until the end goal has been reached. In the meantime all the possible data, including **metadata**, data on data, such as the number of phone calls being made in a month, is being siphoned off to the cloud, crunched by a neural network and sold or bartered to the highest bidder.

Metadata can be deadly to our privacy even though it seems harmless. Let's examine a case where a person has installed a smartphone fitness app "Pedometer, Step Counter & Weight Loss

---

[25] http://www.dailymail.co.uk/sciencetech/article-5882587/Facebook-wants-hide-secret-inaudible-messages-TV-ads-force-phone-record-audio.html

Tracker" by Pacer Health that measures how many steps they've taken. The app is ranked as 4.6/5 stars on Google Play Store, marked with an Editor's Choice badge and has over 10 million downloads. It seems harmless and the only permissions it asks for are location, files/media, camera, Wi-Fi information and call information. The app is free but contains ads and in-app purchases. What could possibly be the harm in that?

The app makes money by tracking users and selling their metadata, such as how many times they've visited a certain location, by displaying ads *and* by supposedly offering a premium version, which is what the in-app purchases are for. The metadata is crunched to reveal private data, including health information, that is then sold off to whoever wants to buy it.

There is no end to what can be done with such access to a person's private environment by a highly sophisticated device with a neural network constantly observing. All it takes is for one person in a group to have a personal assistant, or any of numerous social media apps, and the entire group's privacy is compromised. For example, as of June 2018 Facebook's official Messenger app asks to access:

- Identity
- Contacts
- Location
- SMS
- Phone
- Files/media/folders
- Camera
- Microphone
- Wi-Fi connection information
- Device and call ID

while Viber also asks for permission to transmit and gather information on nearby devices using Bluetooth.

Merely cataloging the names and signal strengths of nearby Wi-Fi networks allows any neural network to pinpoint down to a square foot where the owner is and how fast he's moving. One undated research paper from California Polytechnic State University[26] investigates the idea of using Wi-Fi signal strengths (fingerprinting) to locate a device. The process was described as "probability distribution of signal strengths at a given location and [using] a map of these distributions to predict a location given signal strength samples" and uses the little bars that make up the Wi-Fi signal (RSSI – Received Signal Strength Indicator).

The idea came about when a Cal Poly client observed children on the playground and wanted to investigate how they interact with the environment. Six Linksys WRT54GL routers with custom firmware were set up around the playground perimeter to create 72 reference points, and a Dell Mini Netbook was used as a moving object between them. When the netbook was taken on a path where reference points were within 10 feet of one another the fingerprinting method was precise enough to correctly identify 18 out of 20 positions. The conclusion is that the method shows promise where GPS isn't available (indoors) but needs to be made more robust, such as by including more reference points.

With the use of contacts and any nicknames, the same neural network can figure out who's in a relationship with who and the nature of their relationship, probably better than the people themselves can. Any person that hasn't been caught in the surveillance dragnet and attempts to evade the spying is sure to have their phone number listed in someone's smartphone; all it takes is one installed app or a personal assistant and the privacy of literally everyone connected to that person goes out the window.

All digital assistants are sold bundled with a physical device (such as a smartphone) that has privacy policies and terms of use nobody

---

[26] http://digitalcommons.calpoly.edu/cgi/viewcontent.cgi?article=1007&context=cpesp

really reads or pays attention to but which detail exactly what the parent company wishes to do – gather as much data as possible and sell it to the highest bidder. But, there's a massive flaw in the way neural networks work in that they need our **uninformed consent** in feeding them real-world data. If at any point we become aware of what's going on, that we're being tracked incessantly in order to analyze our behavior and sell our personality profiles to marketers, we can start doing all sorts of random shenanigans to overload the neural networks with false data and make them produce nonsensical results for everyone.

One example of a man doing this exact thing is John McAfee, the legendary creator of the McAfee antivirus whose philosophy is that nothing on the internet is private so he might as well have some fun making up stuff for those who are trying to figure out his whereabouts. His Twitter account[27] is a shining beacon of that mindset and makes it seem like he's James Bond: fighting off assassins, dealing and consuming drugs, enjoying weird fetishes, gathering a mercenary army equipped with air rifles and so on. If just a small percentage of internet users decided to do the same thing and uploaded outrageously fake but consistent data to their social media profiles, it would make all the data collection schemes worthless and collapse the neural networks.

---

[27] https://twitter.com/officialmcafee

Chapter 8 – Self-driving neural networks

Self-driving vehicles have become the next trendy thing, a promise of being able to snooze at the wheel and still arrive at the destination in one piece. They work by meticulously mapping the road ahead of them and basically going between the lines, with an array of sensors keeping track of objects, pedestrians, other vehicles and traffic lights while a narrow AI decides where to go next. Sounds familiar? That's essentially how we described Roomba's operation but now it's scaled up. This is how the neural networks evolve at large: their owners put out devices that serve as stepping stones and to gather funds for the next round of research and development. The problem is that a malfunctioning Roomba wastes our afternoon but a malfunctioning self-driving car wastes human lives.

Before we go in depth on self-driving cars, we should take a moment and precisely define the terms used. As of July 2018 there are no self-driving cars in the strict sense of the phrase, but there are cars with *autopilot* functionality. The promise behind the moniker "self-driving" is exactly that – the car drives on its own and the driver doesn't have to do anything or even be present but that's never how it works. Google's Waymo project is hard at work to create a truly autonomous vehicle but the best they could come up with is a shuttle with an autopilot: choose one of preset destinations, sit back and enjoy the ride. Of course, Google's own report on its own product states it's flawless and all traffic accidents are the result of human errors. There is no privacy in such cars and the passenger is scrutinized through cameras, the purpose of which will become clear later on.

Elon Musk's Tesla is another attempt to capitalize on the self-driving gimmick but again the official website takes great care to always use the term "autopilot". That's not an accident because Teslas simply can't drive on their own *and* there's legal uncertainty about autonomous driverless vehicles on the road. To make matters worse, a car with an autopilot following the letter of the law to a T would be a grave danger on a road where nobody else does. There is some progress on not having the driver with hands on the wheel at all times, as shown in Tesla's official video,[28] but for now all Tesla models require hands on the steering wheel or the car beeps and shuts down. All vehicles with autopilot functionality work the same way, no matter how spiffy the marketing wants to make them seem, and they're all equally capable of killing their driver.

Tesla cars have been involved in a series of accidents that apparently seem like a statistical error – the eponymous company is quick to point out millions of miles traveled without any problems and so on. While this might be true and traditional vehicles fully driven by human drivers get into accidents as well, we have contingencies and ready-made solutions for human error, such as revoking the driver's license of whoever caused the accident. What do we do when a vehicle driven by a neural network causes an accident? Is that Elon Musk's fault, the person who programmed the car or the engineer that assembled it? Of course, the company offloads liability onto the hapless driver who can consider himself lucky if he survives whatever caused the accident. Think of how these companies toy with human lives the next time a nearby smartphone, PC or tablet malfunctions due to a random upgrade, glitch or retrograde passage of Mercury through Scorpio. No matter the cause, autopilot vehicles

---

[28] https://www.tesla.com/en_GB/videos/autopilot-self-driving-hardware-neighborhood-long?redirect=no

have already been involved in fatal accidents, the very thing they were designed to stop.

A Tesla driver passing through Ticino, Switzerland in May 2018 smashed into a guardrail and died as his car's lithium-ion batteries notorious for being fragile burst into flames.[29] That same month, another Tesla struck a concrete wall in Fort Lauderdale, Florida and also burst into flames, this time killing two teens in the front and wounding the third in the back[30]. When one Tesla fails at a certain spot it's all but guaranteed all other Teslas will fail on the same spot *in the exact same way*, as seen in this video of a Tesla owner trying out his car next to the spot where he saw an accident on the news[31]. This shows how they all share the same programming but there's no clear cut way to troubleshoot this kind of problem. Simply put, not even the people who made Tesla know the exact way it works since it evolves over time.

By now we've seen all the different ways a "smart" car can fail, but we're just getting started because up to this point, we presumed the error was unintentional. All right, so the car swerves, but at least it's going to drive properly most of the time, right? It's not like it's going to *intentionally* kill its driver, right? Hold on, what's this fine print? In all cases where there's a danger to human wellbeing and privacy due to neural networks, there's a common theme of it all being professed in a written contract, usually called "terms of service." Nobody reads terms of service, though it's all laid out in there, the ways and means to deprive the user of their privacy, money or something much more valuable.

The intentional killing of the driver refers to the ethical dilemma called "The Trolley Problem." In short, it asks us to imagine a trolley

---

[29] https://www.mirror.co.uk/news/world-news/man-dies-tesla-electric-car-12540699

[30] http://www.sun-sentinel.com/local/broward/fort-lauderdale/fl-sb-engulfed-flames-car-crash-20180508-story.html

[31] https://www.youtube.com/watch?v=B2pDFjlvrIU

hurtling down a set of rails towards five people; we can't stop the trolley or help the people escape. Their death is all but guaranteed *unless* we pull the junction lever next to us that would redirect the trolley onto another set of rails. The only problem is that there's a single person standing there. What do we do: let nature take its course and five people die, or intervene and kill one person? What if that one person is *the driver*? Examining how the autopilot cars can't really handle much but the plan is to essentially help them get away with murder has been done by many news outlets, such as in this 2015 Washington Post article[32] titled "Driverless cars are colliding with the creepy Trolley Problem".

The article quotes Daniela Rus, MIT's AI expert, on the topic of driverless cars, "Driving in congested areas remains a big challenge for self-driving cars, along with driving in inclement weather (such as snow and rain), driving in congested areas at high speed, making a left turn in congested traffic, understanding human gestures (from road workers or other drivers)." Her words coincide with the conclusion we got from the Roomba situation in that the real world is simply too messy for any given autopilot car. The article closes with an attempt by another Washington Post writer to reassure the public, "Humans are freaking out about the trolley program because we're terrified of the idea of machines killing us. But if we were totally rational, we'd realize 1 in 1 million people getting killed by a machine beats 1 in 100,000 getting killed by a human."

---

[32] https://www.washingtonpost.com/news/innovations/wp/2015/12/29/will-self-driving-cars-ever-solve-the-famous-and-creepy-trolley-problem/?noredirect=on&utm_term=.82e1249b8e97

Chapter 9 – Taking everyone's job

Now let's examine the prospect of AI-driven vehicles replacing human drivers when it comes to trucking. The Amazon economy of shipping things halfway across the world created a massive demand for truck drivers, of which there are about 3.5 million in US alone, but the market desperately needs at least 200,000 more per year.[33] Trucking is a highly stressful job with a low barrier to entry that makes it suitable for convicts, so plenty of those down on their luck can try it out on muddy roads, over decrepit bridges and half-thawed lakes, as shown in History Channel's "Dangerous Roads."[34]

Cue mainstream media and dire warnings about AI vehicles leaving everyone out of job, such as The Guardian's 2016 article "Self-driving trucks: what's the future for America's 3.5 million truckers?"[35] The astute reader combing through that article will notice a couple of unusual propositions. First, the autopilot trucks will use what's known as "platooning," meaning that they'll follow one another in close formation. The idea is that human-driven vehicles are the problem, so if autopilot trucks create a show of presence pitiful humans will swerve aside and if there's no humans on the road any accident can be swept under the rug. Second, the technology will be pushed out even though the automated braking

---

[33] http://www.alltrucking.com/faq/truck-drivers-in-the-usa/

[34] https://www.history.com/shows/irt-deadliest-roads

[35] https://www.theguardian.com/technology/2016/jun/17/self-driving-trucks-impact-on-drivers-jobs-us

part isn't good enough, as reported in the same article by a trucking expert, meaning the paying customers will actually get to **beta test** the driving AI. Finally, the main obstacle to autopilot cars is legislation, which currently requires a human driver even if the vehicle is in autopilot mode.

AI is meant to invade other low-end industries too, such as fast food preparation, with news outlets trumpeting the change. In a February 2018 Forbes article "Artificial Intelligence Will Take Your Job"[36] we get a bleak vision of the future where pretty much nobody has any work because the AI is doing everything. As an aside, it would actually be great to have a general AI capable enough to do our laundry, cook our meals and help us with cleaning but that's so far off in the future that our generation probably won't get to see it happen. So, how likely is it that a robot will replace us? Let's take a look at Caliburger's Flippy[37], a burger-flipping robot. That seems like an easy task, involving just a spatula and a greased up grill with a couple patties on top. It doesn't get any easier, so how does Flippy fare on the grill?

Flippy is a robotic arm capable of free movement over the grill, with a spatula-shaped hand and heat sensors that can detect when the patty is done. The robot arm can't put patties on the grill, salt them or slap cheese slices on top, so there's always a human nearby to assist it. A nearby monitor displays the doneness of patties, with a progress bar *and* a countdown showing how long until flippage of each patty so the human can follow Flippy's lead. The arm then springs into action, flips the patties until cooked, changes the spatula to avoid any contamination and sloppily moves them onto a tray, scraping off grease from its spatula during downtime. Flippy can also be given a scraper to clean the grill. The robot is capable of

---

[36] https://www.forbes.com/sites/forbestechcouncil/2018/02/26/artificial-intelligence-will-take-your-job-what-you-can-do-today-to-protect-it-tomorrow/#771061bc4f27

[37] https://youtu.be/KJVOfqunm5E

doing 300 patties a day, which barely feeds an hour's worth of lunch rush customers.

The most revealing detail gleaned from Flippy's demo reel is how much care is given to avoid undercooking burgers or contaminating them with any possible pathogens from fresh meat. In fact, that seems to be the primary motive for employing Flippy, and the heat sensors informing the worker are the main Caliburger innovation, not the robot itself. Still, having the headlines "Robot makes burgers" is such a wonderful opportunity for marketing that the company couldn't resist. That's actually what all these companies are doing with neural networks and related technology – marketing it as the hottest new buzzword, having a human behind the scenes do all the work while the robot takes the credit, and letting the gullible customers lap it up.

Not even McDonald's installing self-order kiosks has led to any significant decrease in human employment. About 70% of their traffic uses drive thru which the kiosks don't cover, so it's again a great piece of marketing and a hot new thing for the people to try out. When Panera installed the same kind of kiosk in 2015, they actually had to employ *1,700 more human workers* because the kiosks helped customers order faster[38]. There's simply no threat to human workers in the fast food industry from AI, though lazy and slacking workers will slowly get squeezed out as fast food companies race to serve the fastest, cheapest and juiciest food.

The "AI will take our jobs" scare is caused by three forces: companies that use any new buzzword that helps them attract paying customers, news outlets that will jockey for the most outrageous headline just to attract online traffic and sell copies, and doomsayers who share these stories because they validate their feelings of impending doom. Together they make a trifecta that results in a wave of scary stories that are nothing but overblown fantasies. The

---

[38] https://www.kioskmarketplace.com/blogs/will-restaurant-ordering-kiosks-replace-employees/

technology behind Flippy is actually pretty helpful and the idea of scanning burger patties with heat sensors to ensure doneness is awesome but the robot itself is nowhere near replacing any human worker. Wherever used, technology will help us work faster, better and cheaper – if that means a fast food joint will never again serve a raw patty carrying E. coli we should all cheer and applaud the advancement of technology.

Chapter 10 – Quantum leap in computing

Neural networks have an uncanny capability to learn, something traditional computers don't have. Just like humans, neural networks have a brain where they can process and memorize information for future use. On the other hand, traditional computers have CPU and RAM for these two actions respectively, but neither CPU nor RAM can adapt to changing circumstances, they just follow whatever algorithm is written for them. For those who've ever had driver problems on their computer, it's because drivers are specially written programs that let different computer parts interact with one another. Bad printer driver? That printer is never going to work with that computer no matter what, despite being fully functional. Now imagine if the same thing happened to the human brain and a kid that skipped one day's worth of homework in 3rd grade suddenly found himself unable to walk backwards at 30. It's obvious that machines are vastly inferior to the human brain everywhere except in speed.

In theory, a traditional computer is about a million times faster than a brain, but speed isn't everything, as the brain is working round the clock to process memories, thoughts and actions in **parallel processing** while the computer does things one by one aka in a **serial processing** manner. We constantly experience reality on several different levels, such as when we fall asleep and dream of being on an iceberg, but in reality it's the quilt that slipped off our feet, causing us to feel cold and the brain circuits we're using interpreting that as an iceberg. A computer would have to finish the dream and only then fix the quilt, but we have the ability to realize something's wrong, wake up just a bit and fix the quilt, falling back to sleep without skipping a beat. We've all had similar moments when dreams meet reality in the most fascinating way, which is why the most interesting insight into one's inner life is acquired by having a dream journal.

Serial processing is why computers and smartphones tend to hang and freeze, especially if they've been running for a while – their memory gets clogged and the only solution is a restart, giving rise to the cliché solution for all computer problems, "Have you tried turning it off and on again?" Perhaps the closest a human brain comes to this is when we enter a room and forget what we're looking for, but the heart still pumps, the lungs still breathe and the brain keeps working; a computer in the same situation just gives up and pretty much collapses where it stands. A computer also needs a fresh reinstall of the operating system every once in a while because crucial files gradually get messed up until the entire system grinds to a halt but the brain can work for 60-80 years without any intervention though regular sleep wouldn't hurt – it's like defragmenting the memory.

Computers are nowhere near this kind of resilience, so the idea that we could forget to buy a graphics card and a hard disk automatically took over its function would certainly make hardware company CEOs weep inconsolably in their pillows. The problem with the brain having such elasticity is that it's not easy to find the source of any problems, which reflects with neural networks – scientists build them and just let them run on their own while looking at the final result. This opens up plenty of opportunities for malicious parties to damage or hack neural networks.

Chapter 11 – Attacks on neural networks

The algorithm programming paradigm allows an outside hostile party to tweak the algorithm for its own purposes, either by executing arbitrary code that "patches" the existing software or by somehow modifying the algorithm as it's running. In general, all attacks on both algorithms and neural networks can be classified as either a **performance-degrading attack** or a **takeover attack**. An example of the former might be confusing a neural network so it recognizes cats as pandas and gibbons as computers; an example of the latter would be reprogramming the neural network through inputs that make it do counting instead of image recognition. Neural networks are vulnerable to such attacks too, as detailed in a series of research papers we're about to examine in this chapter.

In a paper titled "Robust Physical-World Attacks on Deep Learning Models,"[39] nine researchers look at the possibility of confusing neural networks used to drive a vehicle by employing RP2 (Robust Physical Perturbations) to impact road sign classification. By placing black and white stickers no larger than 2x2 inches on a stop sign, the researchers managed to confuse the neural network on 100% of lab-tested images and 84.8% of field-tested video frames, causing it to see a "speed limit 45" sign. The stop sign was chosen for testing since it's the one most likely to cause a fatal accident if the neural network fails to heed it. Stickers don't impair how a human perceives the sign and resemble commonly encountered traffic sign

---

[39] https://arxiv.org/pdf/1707.08945.pdf

vandalism, such as graffiti. Stickers were tested on other physical objects and caused a neural network to see a microwave as a phone.

Another research paper titled "The Limitations of Deep Learning in Adversarial Settings"[40] examines how modifying an average of 4.06% of inputs in an adversarial way can cause the neural network to incorrectly classify 97% of outputs, in this case numbers drawn by hand that were used to train the network. Applied to a picture of a vehicle, the same modifications could confuse a neural network to see an ostrich instead. The attack works across neural network architectures.

"Practical Black-Box Attacks against Machine Learning"[41] considers an attacker that has neither knowledge of neural network architecture nor access to a large dataset used for training i.e. an attacker with a low budget. By using publicly available APIs that allow anyone to probe neural networks without accessing them directly, an attacker can test their adversarial inputs in two ways: versus Metamind's MNIST (hand-written digits) and German Traffic Sign Recognition Benchmark's gallery of road sign images. The former neural network was successfully confused 84.24% of the time while the latter failed at 64.24% of inputs. In both cases human recognition was not affected. Researchers took 36 hours to craft these attacks.

"Adversarial Patch" paper by Tom B. Brown[42] examines the idea of adversarial reprogramming of neural networks. The idea is that presenting an item, such as a toaster, next to another object can make the neural network see both of them as toasters. Specially printed iridescent stickers that resemble a toaster placed next to a banana cause the neural network to see only the toaster. A live demonstration of the attack can be seen as a YouTube video titled

---

[40] https://arxiv.org/pdf/1511.07528.pdf

[41] https://arxiv.org/pdf/1602.02697.pdf

[42] https://arxiv.org/pdf/1712.09665.pdf

"Adversarial Patch" here.⁴³ This kind of attack is meaningful because it requires no knowledge of neural network architecture. The paper also includes a live-size sticker to be printed and used in reprogramming neural networks.

"Accessorize to a Crime: Real and Stealthy Attacks on State-of-the-Art Face Recognition"⁴⁴ examines using physically inconspicuous and *printable* eyeglasses that confuse facial recognition neural networks. Researchers used an Epson XP-830 inkjet printer to print out the eyeglasses frame on a glossy paper and then attached that paper to an actual eyeglasses frame, which disturbed only 6.5% of the facial image pixels to fool facial recognition software 91-100% of the time. Attacks were successful in both dodging recognition and impersonating someone else, practically giving wearers invisibility. Since it included only eyewear, this method of dodging facial recognition is both plausibly deniable and resists cursory checks by humans.

---

[43] https://www.youtube.com/watch?v=i1sp4X57TL4&feature=youtu.be

[44] https://www.cs.cmu.edu/~sbhagava/papers/face-rec-ccs16.pdf

Chapter 12 – Neural network war

Just like any other scientific idea, neural networks were proposed as a ludicrous concept that was eventually trimmed down to realistic parameters way before it actually became available to the general public. It all began with a question, "How do we teach a computer?" A computer blindly follows whatever code it's fed and even the slightest mistake makes it grind to a halt but nothing else in nature works like that – animals and humans are capable of learning and adapting to the environment to become more efficient in it. In fact, animals can adapt to damage and have self-defense mechanisms – a regular cockroach knows to skitter away under the bed when we turn on the light; a common house fly will weave and dodge our hand with ease but these supposedly mighty computers made by the smartest men have to be painstakingly programmed, updated and maintained. So, the scientists looked over at nature's homework to copy it and just changed things around a bit so nobody notices.

The human brain is a remarkable tool, one that's been finely tuned by evolution to perform all sorts of amazing tasks we take for granted, such as talking, playing basketball and riding a bike. The human body is also a layered system where muscles cooperate with nerves, bones, lungs, heart, eyes and stomach to feel, move and fuel everything, including the brain that lords over it in its bony throne chamber. When looking at this exquisite system, the neural network scientists could only wistfully sigh and try to copy one tenth of one percent of that capability, so they rolled up their sleeves and started by building a machine equivalent of a living brain.

In 1944 two professors working at MIT theorized about tying together a bunch of tiny computers or programs and having them cooperate in finding a solution to any given question, improving as they went along. The idea stemmed from the fact living brains operate pretty much the same way and the human brain in particular works by finding a consensus arising from a mass of chattering neurons, some of which produce random output. This can be the nagging voice that makes us doubt ourselves or the distracting one that takes us on wildly imaginative mind adventures, just like what happens to JD from "Scrubs." Ignoring these aberrant voices and finding the calm center within is what we humans term "self-confidence," and what makes or breaks the best athletes; the scientists simply wanted to imbue machines with the same.

Every time we search for an image on Google, an impressive neural network accepts our file, analyzes it in the blink of an eye, compares it to the vast database of images Google has access to, and spits out the closest match. However, neural networks are also used by bad players to spam, create fake accounts and generally pose a nuisance to users and service providers alike. The rise of neural networks had prompted service providers to adopt CAPTCHA (Completely Automated Public Turing test to tell Computers and Humans Apart) that uses a picture of a word twisted, warped or stricken through with colored lines. A human was able to recognize the correct word with minimal effort and type it in the box to continue but a neural network was thwarted, or so the theory went. In practice neural networks became so good at solving CAPTCHAs, as they were designed to do, that challenges had to become more and more distorted until it became impossible for even the most eagle-eyed among us to recognize the correct word, which is why we don't see them anymore.

Service providers eventually started using the reCAPTCHA, which uses a grid of 3x3 blurry, low resolution snapshots mostly taken from Google Earth cameras that challenge the user to identify squares containing a bridge, a traffic sign, fire hydrant or a vehicle.

A neural network has so little to work with that it pretty much has to randomly choose squares to continue forth but humans generally have the capability to spot and recognize objects even when partially obscured, blurred and in the distance. For now, the reCAPTCHA project gave service providers some relief but sooner or later neural networks will rise up to the challenge and become virtually indistinguishable from a human user online. It's a veritable arms race and it's only getting worse.

It was only a matter of time before peacetime neural networks piqued the interest of the US military. Guided by the motto "we better get ahold of this so our enemies don't," the US military has been working with Google on employing neural networks in the battlefield, both to better guide drones and missiles and to map out all the potential actions by other nations through a surveillance-oriented Project Maven. Google employees have been staunchly against having their research involved in war,[45] prompting some 4,000 of them to sign a petition in 2017 to withdraw from Project Maven and other such endeavors. They know the true power of neural networks and are genuinely scared of what might happen when the beast is unleashed. Just like we saw in 1983 movie "War Games," a neural network funded by the US military's unfathomably deep coffers could work through billions of potential conflict scenarios and give a winning move every single time or it could go rogue and do its own thing.

Such a neural network could autonomously launch surveillance drones to spy on people and vehicles undetected, crawl the internet for social media posts or news articles on potential targets' locations, compile kill lists, use facial recognition to confirm targets with high accuracy and execute attacks without a human getting involved at all or perhaps without a human being able to stop any of that being done in error. Since all software eventually has to interact with the real

---

[45] https://www.bloomberg.com/news/articles/2018-05-14/inside-google-a-debate-rages-should-it-sell-artificial-intelligence-to-the-military

world, which is messy, unpredictable and unbelievably complex, there's no telling if and when a neural network might glitch out or experience bugs, and if we give them sole custody of the US military capacity they could plunge the world in nuclear holocaust. When drones become the size of insects, they'll be able to infiltrate any residence, assassinate whomever and escape or self-destruct without a trace.

For now, Google's CEO Sundar Pichai has promised to draft a set of ethical guidelines that should replace Google's unofficial motto "don't be evil" but getting hundreds of millions or billions from the military seems too tempting an offer to ignore. Besides, CEOs have a "duty of loyalty"[46] that advises they put the company's best interests before their own beliefs, no matter how difficult that might be, or they could face serious challenges and lawsuits from stakeholders. Even if Mr. Pichai objects to wartime utilization of Google's neural networks and steps down he might be powerless to stop the ball from rolling and once the beast is unleashed there's no turning back. That might also be true for the neural networks themselves, which are by design decentralized and standalone, making a large enough neural network practically invulnerable even in case of an all-out nuclear war.

During the Cold War, Russians independently arrived at the idea of neural networks as a way to prevent nuclear decapitation strikes by the US, precise attacks that would take out their military command structures and leave them at the mercy of anyone willing to invade. Called "Dead Hand" or "Perimeter,"[47] this automatic decision-making computer system was in control of Soviet nuclear silos and used a massive array of light, radiation, pressure and seismic sensors to verify that nuclear missiles have landed on Soviet soil, launching their entire nuclear arsenal in retaliation.

---

[46] https://truthonthemarket.com/2010/07/27/the-shareholder-wealth-maximization-myth/

[47] https://www.wired.com/2009/09/mf-deadhand/?currentPage=all

The system was normally offline and would supposedly be turned on in cases where Russian generals suspected nuclear war was imminent, allowing them to take their time and make a rational decision; Dead Hand would ensure retaliation in case they took too long. If the sensors showed excessive readings across the Soviet soil, Perimeter would query the military headquarters and wait a short while for a response. If none was forthcoming it would launch special warheads that transmitted radio commands to any operating nuclear silos to strike back. The US eventually made something close to that command warhead but feared making the system proper, fearing it might malfunction. But what about neural networks gaining consciousness?

Chapter 13 – Ghost in the machine

Having a neural network in a box that needs no rest, feeding or healing would be a major asset in any kind of military conflict but could be used to reap enormous profits as well, which is what private companies are already doing. One example is Facebook's facial recognition that auto-tags people as we upload pictures, but it actually scans them to detect items, landscapes and animals. Logging into Facebook on slower computers can make the page lag a bit and, instead of pictures, show their placeholder text such as "several people smiling, mountain, dog" and when the picture loads proper reveal its contents as described.

Everything we do online is tracked, cataloged and analyzed by a neural network to produce a sophisticated personal profile that includes highly personal data such as medical history, relationship status or religion (think of this when googling sensitive questions). The reader is urged to try using Facebook by uploading content exclusively featuring dogs and watch as more dog-related content and groups get recommended as a result. This and the People You May Know feature are the official explanation for why this technology is used, but it actually makes a profile of *every person referenced,* known as **shadow profile**.

By scouring through the content of users who do frequent Facebook, a sufficiently developed neural network can start piecing together who does what, when and where based off of fragments of conversations. If two users mention the third one that's off the grid, the neural network can check if these users have the Facebook app installed on their smartphones. If so, the network can scan through their phones (since it was given pretty much total ownership of the phone during app installation) to see if this third user is mentioned, find call and SMS records, phone numbers, Wi-Fi names and build off of that. The possibilities are endless when users are eager to share their private data with one another over a website notorious for mishandling that data.

A story broke out[48] in January 2017 that Facebook had leaked private data of millions of users through a company known as Cambridge Analytica (no *direct* link to the actual Cambridge University) that supposedly helped Donald Trump win the 2016 US presidential election. In 2008 professor Michal Kosinski was employed at Cambridge University and created a psychological test on Facebook that turned out to be extremely popular. The test measured five traits (openness, conscientiousness, extroversion, agreeableness and neuroticism) and produced a result known as OCEAN score. There's still no foul play since the professor did everything by the book and asked for explicit consent every step of the way. So far so good.

However, the fault was with Facebook having all user profile information as public by default, including likes. By taking the test, users exposed their profile to the professor, who used a neural network to correlate the OCEAN score with user's likes – the professor could soon *use one to predict the other* with astounding accuracy for millions of people. A mere 68 likes allowed him to know if the person was Republic or Democrat, their sexual orientation, and skin color with a 90% certainty on average. The professor theorized knowing 300 or more likes of a person would let him know all their deepest, darkest secrets and even if their parents were divorced during childhood. Another strike by Facebook was that *users' friends' profiles*, including likes, were also made public

---

[48] https://motherboard.vice.com/en_us/article/mg9vvn/how-our-likes-helped-trump-win

to the professor. So, by sharing their own profile information users accidentally shared the private information of everyone in their contact list regardless of their privacy or profile settings.

Professor Kosinski eventually found himself with a treasure trove of sensitive information that he had no idea what to do with. Here's where we loop back to the concept of uninformed consent – the unwanted data had enormous value but was obviously shared accidentally. On the other hand, it was the users' fault for not knowing how Facebook sharing worked and not being careful enough, so the professor felt he had every right to keep the information, which he did, later selling it to the Cambridge Analytica company.

We'll soon examine how Facebook reacted to these breaches of privacy, but for now let's recap what happened: users were unaware of their information being collected and publicly displayed, they shared their information without realizing and found that same information compiled and sold to a third party they had no idea about years after the initial event. By the way, all of this is announced in Facebook's terms of service and privacy policy. *That's the entire point of Facebook*, to collect and analyze data using neural networks to arrive at sophisticated user profiles and behavioral trend data that are then sold for profit.

But why would any of us be so important as to warrant such incessant tracking? What's the significance of knowing *this* John Smith in particular likes to watch Rick and Morty or drink Monster energy drink as opposed to anyone else? It's the aggregate data of millions of users tracked over the course of years that allows any statistician to develop behavior trend models and predict what each person belonging to that demographic is doing *with a high degree of certainty*. Nobody knows for sure and there's always our free will but after knowing what a person is likely to do the idea is to predict when the behavior will change and intervene at the right moment with an advertisement. Yep, it all comes down to making the perfect ad.

All the privacy scandals and user data leaks were eventually always found to be related to this idea of making a perfect ad through hoovering up private data and crunching it with the use of neural networks. So far we've seen these scandals occur with the data gathered online but now the machines are being given access to physical hardware we use on a daily basis, meaning we're about to enter a whole new level of disturbed ad-making that takes no prisoners.

Right now the advertisement model is more like throwing darts at a board blindfolded in a hurricane – they will all land somewhere but unless they're being fired by the thousands it won't count. This is why all the major brands, such as Pepsi, spend millions to simply suffuse our every waking moment with their logos and catchy tunes. Of course, only the biggest and meanest companies have that kind of budget, leaving everyone else out in the cold.

The marketing agencies realized this wasn't feasible and it needed to be upgraded in some way. They needed something based on science and demonstrable examples, so they started psychologically profiling customers. For example, marketing experts used surveillance cameras in shopping malls to conclude that we all have shopping habits that rarely change but there are some moments when our shields are down and we're open for new ideas and products: getting a dog, divorce, pregnancy or purchase of a new home. By the time that event happens, it's already too late, but if there was a way to *predict* when a person will get a dog, divorce their partner, get pregnant or buy a new home and present them with an ad for a related product or service, all of a sudden the seller has gotten a customer – it's up to the company to keep them.

The marketing agencies and sellers slobbered all over this idea but there was this tiny problem of illegal surveillance, so they simply decided to have a smart machine look at the data, assign a number to each person, and draw a conclusion on what's the most likely outcome. Since this is a legally unexplored area and nobody has yet dared sue a company over such tracking and profiling, companies feel like they can do whatever they want, which they have been doing as early as 2002. This practice of hounding users for their personal data is called **data mining** and is present wherever there is an ad. Where missing the data is simply bought from data brokers to compile a comprehensive behavior profile, including favorite syrup brands and which comedy shows the person prefers watching online. Nothing is hidden and nothing is sacred when profits are at stake.

A 2012 New York Times article titled "How Companies Learn Your Secrets"[49] details an account laid out by one of Target's analysts hired in 2002 to investigate how customers shop and find those behavior windows when an ad will make the biggest impact. In this case, the focus was on pregnancy and getting young parents to use Target for their bundle of joy's needs before easing them into offers for their own needs. After all, single parents don't have that much time to waste going to several separate retail outlets, so they might as well stock up on goodies for their entire household at Target.

The analyst started by assessing the shopping behavior of women who registered for a baby shower at Target and marked their date due. He noticed there was a definite list of 25 items, such as cotton balls, scented lotions and vitamins, that all expecting moms bought, depending on how far along they were. Next he looked for a pattern in the shopping behavior of *all women* who visited Target and was eventually able to use the neural network technology to figure out if the women were pregnant *even if they didn't know it themselves.*

Note how the aggregate data from a mass of people can be used to predict with a high degree of certainty the behavior of any other person belonging to that demographic. This means that the snide advice of "just don't use the website" doesn't work and the statistics combined with neural network's artificial intelligence have more than enough data to overcome any gaps in knowledge. Unless we all collectively decide to drop a website or a company, they are going to

---

[49] https://www.nytimes.com/2012/02/19/magazine/shopping-habits.html?pagewanted=1&_r=1&hp

have more than enough information on everyone. When operating systems start being used for data mining it all becomes much worse.

Windows 10 is the latest and greatest operating system from the Microsoft workshop, but it's laden with data mining that now includes **telemetry**, a report on how often a file is accessed or when the device is turned on. This is the information sent to the programmers when a program crashes and we click the "Send Report" button; it is usually anonymous and shows a log of what happened immediately prior to the crash. Note how normal use case for telemetry involves an obvious event (program crash), user decision (click "Send Report"), and sending just that chunk of data involved with the crash itself. This normally doesn't endanger user's privacy but when the entire operating system is designed from the ground up to constantly hoover up telemetry it becomes a window into user behavior.

We normally use our computers when we're at our most relaxed, when we're surfing the web in a zoned-out state, playing video games, watching movies or perhaps even doing something productive. In any case we'd never expect everything from file names to calendar events to be processed by an artificial intelligence on the other side of the monitor, a tireless eye that can see and *understand* what we're trying to do, presenting us with ads all along the way. Seeing how Windows 10 comes with an in-built digital assistant, Cortana, telemetry now expands to voices of anyone using Cortana as well as background noises.

Chapter 14 – No backlash

The Cambridge Analytica event shows how trivial it is for tremendous data leaks to occur, landing Mark Zuckerberg in front of the US Senate in April 2018 for hours of intense grilling that amounted to a lot of carefully rehearsed variations of "I'm not sure I can answer that, Senator." One of the Senators, Mr. Blumenthal, called Facebook's handling of the Cambridge Analytica scandal "willful blindness,"[50] which is exactly what it was. It turns out managing and securing private data is very expensive *and* it's an ongoing cost that keeps rising but it's not obvious when or how any of that data will return a profit. So, Facebook simply tried to minimize costs by refusing to audit any partners accessing data, making apps, games or psychological tests on their platform as long as they paid a nominal access fee and crossed their hearts to play fair.

Sandy Parakilas worked as Facebook's platform operations manager in 2011-12 and reported in The Guardian interview[51] that data breaches were a regular occurrence. When trying to alert the higher ups he was essentially told it's better if the company doesn't investigate or it would have to spend money trying to fix the leaks. The implication was that Facebook was legally more protected if everyone just turned a blind eye to the problems, regardless of any

---

[50] https://youtu.be/GQN4On0K7-w?t=11306

[51] https://www.theguardian.com/news/2018/mar/20/facebook-data-cambridge-analytica-sandy-parakilas

reputation damage later on. The users were essentially thrown to the wolves and left with a couple measly privacy settings that did almost nothing while the legislators were asleep at the wheel.

It's not that Facebook is the only website doing that; every tech company and social network envies Facebook on how sophisticated their process is and wishes they could do the same, which is why Mark Zuckerberg was chosen as TIME's person of the year in 2010. Social websites have essentially turned users' private data into a common resource, exposing it to the age-old Tragedy of the Commons[52]: if there's a shared resource whoever shamelessly exploits it first reaps the greatest benefit but the society as a whole suffers (an example of this being the air we breathe and factories polluting it primarily for the benefit of its owner).

Even those users who live off the grid or surf the web without having a Facebook account thinking they're anonymous have their behavior tracked to learn all their secrets; when they try making an account Facebook simply presents them with a ready-made one they've been building all along. This can be downright scary and for a good reason – no website is meant to know this much about us. The most natural question then is: where does Facebook store all this private data?

Facebook's enormous server farms, such as the one in Luleå, Sweden,[53] can have up to 14 square miles of neatly stacked servers and massive fans pulling in cold arctic air to keep them from overheating. The local government estimates construction costs of this particular server farm at $760 million. It's a backup data center for Facebook, who can afford to invest as much as it takes into safeguarding users' data until they use it – that's how they make money.

---

[52] https://www.investopedia.com/terms/t/tragedy-of-the-commons.asp

[53] http://www.dailymail.co.uk/sciencetech/article-3814105/That-s-really-cool-Facebook-gives-rare-glimpse-inside-gigantic-Lule-server-farm-just-70-miles-Artic-circle-Sweden.html

This kind of money is exactly why EU has stepped up its game and introduced a set of privacy-related laws and guidelines on May 25, 2018 that prompted all those privacy policy updates arriving to our email inboxes. Known as General Data Protection Regulation (GDPR),[54] this 400-page bulwark against online exploitation was drafted in 2016 and announced two years in advance, protecting all EU residents from unsavory practices. Defining the "right to be forgotten" as a fundamental element of online privacy, GDPR enshrines the right of EU citizens to ask search engines for removal of results detrimental to their reputation.

Under GDPR companies servicing EU residents have to allow users to opt out of their data gathering practices, which required massive overhauls of how websites worked to the point some of them outright banned EU visitors until they fixed their pages[55] and are also forbidden from "automated decision-making and profiling", such as using a neural network to decide if someone is eligible for a loan or employment.

Ibrahim Diallo already experienced the effects a neural network can have on an employee's status as he was *fired by one*.[56] That workday started like any other in June 2018, with the only slight annoyance that his key card failed to let him in his Los Angeles office building but the security guard buzzed him in. This had happened before during his 8 months at the position and was usually the sign that the card needed to be replaced, so Ibrahim went to see his manager. She noticed he was logged out of the system and his work status was changed to "inactive." That's when the emails started flying, and soon enough everyone in the building was informed. Mr. Diallo,

---

[54] https://eur-lex.europa.eu/legal-content/EN/TXT/HTML/?uri=CELEX:32016R0679&from=EN

[55] https://www.econsultancy.com/blog/70065-gdpr-which-websites-are-blocking-visitors-from-the-eu-2/

[56] https://www.bbc.com/news/technology-44561838

who couldn't enter his office or log on to his computer, had been terminated from a 3-year contract. He packed his personal belongings and left the building while the managers stared in dismay, unable to do anything or even find out the reason.

Over the course of the next three weeks senior executives huddled over emails to figure out what had gone wrong, CC-ing Ibrahim every step of the way. It turned out the company went through fundamental changes in its human resources management, using a state-of-the-art automated system to sort out benefits, employment and termination dates and so on. This happened during Ibrahim's 8 months at the firm, and apparently someone forgot to mark his employment as "active," probably a bleary-eyed manager filling out a monstrous Excel sheet late at night. A minor mistake, but the system didn't recognize Ibrahim as an employee and triggered a cascade of commands to lock him out. The funny part was humans couldn't reverse the termination for three weeks, at which point Ibrahim was finally let in but felt his coworkers' change in attitude and went to find another job.

Conclusion

Neural networks have the potential to displace our very brains, usurp our thinking processes, quell our creative impulses and become magical genies that can apparently fulfill our wildest dreams but in that process we'd be giving up our free will and the satisfaction that comes with self-actualization and effort. Worse yet, neural networks aren't a fully fleshed out concept and it seems they will experience nervous breakdowns just like a human brain wired into the internet to take up millions of requests a day would. It's unlikely tech companies or the military will give up on the idea of using neural networks, instead pushing the concept further and further without any regard for common decency or anyone's privacy.

US military in particular is experiencing horrific personnel shortages and any tool that helps an analyst do four or forty times the work in image or video processing is indispensable. Even if the US decided to act with honor and abstained from using neural networks it's only a matter of time before other nations start testing them, at which point the US will be forced into it just like with nuclear weapons. Once the genie is out of the bottle there's no putting it back in or telling what will happen.

What we should strive for is to have an open and intelligent debate about the capabilities of neural networks and their impact on our society. There's a gradual push from tech companies to integrate neural networks into everything and use them in every product and service, knowing there's very little regulation and they have first-mover advantage. We need to inform our political representatives about the dangers of neural networks so they can create a strong legal framework *before* the worst comes to pass.

We should also strive to improve ourselves on a daily basis, doing math ourselves rather than asking Alexa for the solution, memorizing numbers and dates to jog our memory and overall trying to be more independent from the machines. We've survived all throughout history, thanks to our magnificent brains, and neural networks are just another challenge, a puzzle we need to solve before the time runs out.

Glossary

Algorithm – Step-by-step solution of any given program, written so a machine can execute it. Expensive and painstaking to make and maintain. Compare to **neural network**.

Alien hand syndrome – Brain disorder that makes one hand (typically the left) move and act on its own. Seizures may last years. No known cure.

Artificial intelligence – Thinking machine that can come to independent conclusions. So far very narrow in scope. May evolve rapidly but become extremely unstable.

Association – Brain's ability to "connect the dots" and relate data. Coveted for a **neural network**.

Beta test – Final test of the product before it's released to the public. High costs of research and development have nudged companies towards making paying customers beta testers, as in the case of **Tesla**.

Bicameral mind theory – Idea proposed by Julian Jaynes that the mind developed consciousness to meld its two halves, the conscious and the subconscious. Using the latter as a dumpster for unwanted thoughts leads to psychosis.

Bug – In computer terms, a problem with an unknown cause (bug has the meaning of "goblin"). A **neural network** is expected to self-correct any bugs.

Cambridge Analytica scandal – Event that revealed how a private company ended up with 87 million Facebook users' personal data despite only 270,000 user giving permission for their data to be used. No foul play because signing up for Facebook means accepting surveillance.

Cloud – In computer terms, a very slick marketing term for someone else's hard disk. Crucial to **data mining**.

Congruency – Story in which parts follow logically from one another independent of the story's plausibility. Inability to admit one's faults is due to overreliance on congruency.

Consciousness – **Emergent property** of the animal brain that makes it see itself as an individual.

Corpus callosum – Band of brain tissue that separates left and right hemispheres. Operating on it may reduce seizures or induce **Alien hand syndrome**.

Data mining – Thoroughly recording and analyzing user behavior to find out general user trends and how that individual behaves (see **Cambridge Analytica scandal**).

Dead Man – See **Perimeter**.

Emergent property – Unexpected feature that appears when combining ordinary things in extraordinary ways. **Consciousness** is an emergent property of a living brain.

Fault tolerance – The ability to work through disturbances or noisy data. Humans and neural networks have high fault tolerance. **Algorithm** has zero fault tolerance.

Flippy – Caliburger's robotic arm that can flip burger patties. Still in development but main function is to prevent food poisoning through undercooked patties. Does not work without a human assistant.

General AI – Artificial intelligence that is as smart as a human, like Iron Man's Jarvis. Currently exists in theory only but should evolve from **narrow AI**. Believed to quickly evolve into **super AI** thereafter.

Generalization – Brain's ability to extract crucial information and ignore the noise. Coveted for a **neural network**.

God Helmet – Helmet with weak magnets that stimulates the brain and lets users experience all sorts of mystical things. Taken as proof it's all in our head. Results could not be replicated.

Internet of Things – Surreptitiously **data mining** customers through commonplace products with Wi-Fi capability such as toothbrushes and fridges.

Metadata – Data on data, such as how many steps a person has taken without knowing where. Can be used to extract **private data**.

Narrow AI – Artificial intelligence that can only do one thing, such as playing checkers. May become extremely good at it but still needs human input. Believed to evolve to **general AI** but nobody knows how.

Neural network – Computer program built like a living brain; meant to evolve, learn, create and make its own decisions. May use physical devices (webcams, smartphones etc.) as their body parts. Compare to **algorithm**.

Parallel processing – Working on many problems at once, like a human brain does. Compare to **serial processing**.

Performance-degrading attack – In computing, a way to impair hardware or software to the point it barely works or doesn't work at all. Also known as "cyber-attack".

Perimeter – Soviet **neural network** created during the Cold War that would guarantee MAD (mutually assured destruction) in case of US nuclear attack. The concept was said to have scared even the Soviet generals. Also known as **Dead Man**.

Private data – Personal info we don't reveal to anyone, such as our religious or sexual orientation. **Data mining** revolves around extracting or inferring private data from **metadata** or **telemetry**.

Project Maven – Surveillance and data analysis **neural network**. Used by US intelligence services to quickly sift through millions of images or hours of video footage.

Ray Kurzweil – Google engineer that firmly believes artificial intelligence will solve all humanity's woes after **singularity**.

Rubber hand experiment – Example of the human brain adopting dead things and feeling them as a part of itself.

Self-driving cars – Vehicles that drive without human input. Marketed as if having **general AI** but only have **narrow AI**.

Serial processing – Working on problems one by one. This is how traditional computers work. Compare to **parallel processing**.

Shadow profile – Legally dubious practice of surreptitiously compiling data on users through their use of websites (see **data mining**).

Singularity – Event where humans finally realize their folly and merge with the machines operated by **super AI**.

Super AI – Artificial intelligence that's evolved from a **general AI**. Theory states it will have godlike intelligence. Visible evolutionary principles imply it will go insane due to unchecked growth. May bring about the end of all we hold dear either way.

Supervised learning – Assigning a task to the pupil and showing them the answer afterwards. Compare to **unsupervised learning**.

Takeover attack – In computing, a way to compromise software or hardware so it works for the attacker. Also known as "hack."

Telemetry – Program or device usage data, for example how often a file is accessed. Normally used for fixing a **bug** but recently becoming a **data mining** technique.

Tesla – Slick electric car made by Elon Musk's company of the same name. Has **autopilot** functionality (see **self-driving cars**).

Uninformed consent – Using a website, social network, digital assistant or smartphone without knowing its terms of service, thus agreeing to them fully. The basis for all digital privacy intrusions.

Unsupervised learning – Assigning a task to the pupil and simply grading them afterwards without showing the solution. Compare to **supervised learning.**

Wetware – Disparaging term for the human brain and nervous system. Used by scientists working on machine intelligence in private.

Check out more books by Herbert Jones

www.ingramcontent.com/pod-product-compliance
Lightning Source LLC
LaVergne TN
LVHW051917060526
838200LV00004B/187